Foundations

Teaching believers the basics of the faith for their spiritual health and strength

Jason DeMars

ISBN: 9781729212523
Imprint: Independently published

CONTENTS

INTRODUCTION

For new Christians it is critical to learn the basics of the Christian faith. We are not Christians by confession only. We are known as Christians by the life that we live on a daily basis. Christians are disciples of Jesus Christ. *"By this shall all men know that ye are my disciples, if ye have love one to another."* (John 13:35) Our lives and the love we have for one another will show that we are Christians. The Biblical faith is marked by growth, sincerity and desire. *"As newborn babes, desire the sincere milk of the word, that ye may grow thereby."* (1 Peter 2:2) As a new Christian Peter defines you as a "newborn babe." That is, you have been born again by the Word and Spirit of God.

This booklet is to be used by pastors and evangelists to instruct believers in the faith by introducing them to the Ten Commandments, the New Birth, the Godhead, the Ordinances and the Lord's Prayer. If believers learn this booklet well it will be a foundation for their faith to build upon and grow.

THE NEW BIRTH

What does it mean to be born again?

"3 Jesus answered him, "Truly, truly, I say to you, unless one is born again he cannot see the kingdom of God." 4 Nicodemus said to him, "How can a man be born when he is old? Can he enter a second time into his mother's womb and be born?" 5 Jesus answered, "Truly, truly, I say to you, unless one is born of water and the Spirit, he cannot enter the kingdom of God. 6 That which is born of the flesh is flesh, and that which is born of the Spirit is spirit." (John 3:3-6)

We cannot enter into the kingdom of God without the new birth. It is a necessity to go to heaven. Without it you are destined for a burning hell. Jesus says when you are born of the flesh your nature is after the flesh and when you are born of the Spirit, your nature will be after the Spirit.

"Therefore we are buried with him by baptism into death: that like as Christ was raised up from the dead by the glory of the Father, even so we also should walk in newness of life." (Romans 6:4)

"Not by works of righteousness which we have done, but according to his mercy he saved us, by the washing of regeneration, and renewing of the Holy Ghost." (Titus 3:5)

Being born again means receiving a new life, the Holy Spirit, and the results are that you're nature and desires are new. If your nature and desires are not new then you have not yet been born of the Spirit. It's critical that you begin with this step. Do not fail to receive the Holy Spirit. You must be converted to the Christian faith by the Spirit of God not by mental assent, but spiritual transformation.

Why do we need the new birth?

"¹ And you hath he quickened, who were dead in trespasses and sins; ² Wherein in time past ye walked according to the course of this world, according to the prince of the power of the air, the spirit that now worketh in the children of disobedience: ³ Among whom also we all had our conversation in times past in the lusts of our flesh, fulfilling the desires of the flesh and of the mind; and were by nature the children of wrath, even as others." (Ephesians 2:1-3)

We have to be born again because our first birth, from our mother, caused us to receive an evil nature that is characterized as being dead in trespasses and sins. We are actually dead to obeying the will and purpose of God. Our nature is one that rebels and rejects God and we actually live and act after the nature of Satan, being in the world, and under his control. We lived according to evil desires and wicked thoughts. These thoughts and actions resulted in being dead and destined to experience the wrath of God in hell fire.

We deserve hell fire because we have sinned against an infinitely holy and righteous God. He requires from us this same holiness, but all men have sinned. Each of us have told a lie or lusted after a woman or broken one of the commands of God. As such we are worthy of punishment.

Our sins must be punished and either we will pay for them in hell or Jesus Christ already paid for them on the cross. Through faith in him and the application of his death on the corss through the new birth we receive grace to be pardoned for our sins.

"4 But God, who is rich in mercy, for his great love wherewith he loved us, 5 Even when we were dead in sins, hath quickened us together with Christ, (by grace you have been saved)" (Ephesians 2:4-5)

The evidence that we have been saved is that God made us alive, gave us the Holy Spirit which results in a new nature and new desires.

LAW AND GRACE

What is the difference between Law and Grace?

"For the law was given by Moses, but grace and truth came by Jesus Christ." (John 1:17)

It is important for us to understand the relationship between the Law of God and the Grace of God. If we fail to properly grasp their relationship we will totally pervert the word of God and we will think that we can "sin, that grace may abound."

"What shall we say then? Shall we continue in sin, that grace may abound?" (Romans 6:1)

"What then shall we say? That the law is sin? By no means! Yet if it had not been for the law, I would not have known sin. For I would not have known what it is to covet if the law had not said, "You shall not covet."" (Romans 7:7)

The Law of Moses was given to reveal the nature and holiness of God (Romans 7:12). Since we are sinners the Law also reveals what sin is. We understand God's nature and then comprehend what is means to sin against him. Because we are sinners the Law condemns us. Yet, the Law was intended to bring us life. (Romans 7:10) But because we are dead in trespasses and sins the Law could not bring life.

The important point I want to emphasize and the reason I am writing this booklet is that the Law brings to us the knowledge of sin. It shows and emphasizes the holiness of God. We need to understand the Law so that we can understand what sin is. As Paul writes, *"For sin shall not have dominion over you: for ye are not under the law, but under grace."* (Romans 6:14) This verse strikes the perfect balance. The Law reveals what sin is. Since we are under grace sin will not have dominion over you. Under the Law the command was given and in the flesh we had to obey the law. There was no "grace" given to enable or empower us to obey. Romans 8:2 says, *"For the law of the Spirit of life in Christ Jesus hath made me free from the law of sin and death."* Since we are born again of the Spirit we have a new nature and a new desire placed within us. Therefore, we are not under the dominion of sin. That is grace. Grace is an enabling power that enables us to overcome the power of sin. We are under grace, that is, we are under the enabling power to live a new and different kind of life. Instead of being under the dominion of the law which leads to sin and death we are under the dominion of the Spirit of life which is in Christ Jesus.

FINAL AUTHORITY

What is the final authority of the Christian faith?

"That ye may be mindful of the words which were spoken before by the holy prophets, and of the commandment of us the apostles of the Lord and Saviour:" (2 Peter 3:2)

The words of the prophets and the commands of the apostles are what we are to remember and follow. We have received these words and commands in the form of a book, called the Scriptures.

"¶6 All scripture is given by inspiration of God, and is profitable for doctrine, for reproof, for correction, for instruction in righteousness: ¹⁷ That the man of God may be perfect, throughly furnished unto all good works." (2 Timothy 3:16-17)

The writings of the prophets and the apostles are given by the inspiration of God and they are the rule and absolute of our faith. We must search all things in the Scriptures and follow precisely the commands of the Scriptures. The Holy Spirit in us will lead us to obedience to the Word of God because it is the Spirit that inspired the word.

"For the prophecy came not in old time by the will of man: but holy men of God spake as they were moved by the Holy Ghost." (2 Peter 1:21)

The Spirit of God moved or drove (Paul says inspired - or breathed upon) the writers of the bible to write what they did. As such we refer to the Bible is our authoritative book, it is not merely a holy book that we memorize and

11

recite as a prayer. The Bible is a book that we read to gain wisdom from, to learn what we believe, to grow in faith and to live our lives by.

"But he answered and said, It is written, Man shall not live by bread alone, but by every word that proceedeth out of the mouth of God." (Matthew 4:4)

We are to live by every word that God speaks, not just a few words, but all his words, meditate on them, memorize them and live them.

THE TEN COMMANDMENTS

"And God spake all these words, saying, I am the LORD thy God, which have brought thee out of the land of Egypt, out of the house of bondage." (Exodus 20:1-2)

This is the introduction to the ten commandments. These are the primary moral laws governing the people of God. They are important for us to understand and follow.

The First Commandment

"Thou shalt have no other gods before me." (Exodus 20:3)

This is not a suggestion or an idea, rather, it is a commandment. This is a law and it means we will be held accountable to this law. This means that we cannot pretend to worship the one true and living God while we worship other gods. It tells us there is one God and he alone is worthy of worship. It also commands us to put him first. For example, if there is a challenge between our families, government, friends or co-workers and our faith in God we must put our God and his commands first.

A god is someone we are to expect all good things from; a bountiful harvest, a beautiful day, health, strength and many other blessings. And when there is distress we take refuge and find peace in our god. Many people take refuge in idols or false gods. What you set your heart on and put your trust in is your god. Whether it be a religious object, a religious leader, a family member or the one true God. In this commandment, the one true God is telling us to put our trust, hope and find refuge in him alone. Don't look towards earthly things for your peace, refuge and to provide good things for you.

Often when people are rich they feel secure and put their trust in the money that they have to protect and give them refuge and peace. They have made money their god. As Jesus tells us we cannot serve both God and money. Either will love the one and hate the other or vice versa. God demands that we place our trust in him not things.

What are we trusting in from our religion? Do we place our trust in a religious leader; perhaps your faith and your authority in your life is a pastor or a prophet? These are not good sources to place your trust. They are men and they sin and fail. They make mistakes and fall short, in fact, if your trust is primarily in a man then you will be disappointed. Are you calling upon an imam like Abolfazl or Ali? Is your trust in them to help you and give you refuge? When you rise from your chair do you call upon an imam? God commands you to have no other gods before him. This means that our expectation for good, our refuge and our trust is in him alone. If men fail you, this is not a problem because your trust is in God not men. If your trust is in men then when they fail you will be distraught and pained.

The Second Commandment

"4 Thou shalt not make unto thee any graven image, or any likeness of any thing that is in heaven above, or that is in the earth beneath, or that is in the water under the earth: 5 Thou shalt not bow down thyself to them, nor serve them: for I the LORD thy God am a jealous God, visiting the iniquity of the fathers upon the children unto the third and fourth generation of them that hate me; 6 And shewing mercy unto thousands of them that love me, and keep my commandments." (Exodus 20:4-6)

God commands his people not to worship carved images. The word carved images signifies pagan idols. This means they are not to make into deities any bird, fish, animal or human likeness. Neither are they to carve an image and claim that this is the LORD your God which the Hebrews did while they were in the wilderness and Moses was upon Mount Sinai.

We must be careful what we, as Christians, place our faith in. Do we put faith in a superstition like "the evil eye" or do we hold as sacred an article that belonged to a man of God? In the book of Acts we find that people took aprons from the body of Paul and laid them on sick people for their healing. This was healing from God, not an apron. Likewise, someone was brought to life as their dead corpse was thrown on top of the bones of Elisha. But do these bones or does the apron become a holy item that we revere? No, they are not to be treated with such holy reverence. Only God himself is to be revered and feared, an object, regardless of what it is should not be treated as an item of trust and faith. God alone deserves our trust and worship.

We worship an invisible and immortal God that is all powerful, all knowing and present everywhere. He is not in the shape of any carved image. God is a jealous God and as the Creator of the world he commands us to worship him only, for that was his purpose in creation, to have a people to have a relationship with in order that they might find their greatest joy in worshipping him. Let's read what the apostle Paul spoke to the philosophers in Athens.

"24 God that made the world and all things therein, seeing that he is Lord of heaven and earth, dwelleth not in temples made with hands; 25 Neither is worshipped with men's hands, as though he needed any thing, seeing he giveth to all life, and breath, and all things; 26 And hath made of one blood all nations of men for to dwell on all the face of the earth, and hath determined the times before appointed, and the bounds of their habitation; 27 That they should seek the Lord, if haply they might feel after him, and find him, though he be not far from every one of us: 28 For in him we live, and move, and have our being; as certain also of your own poets have said, For we are also his offspring. 29 Forasmuch then as we are the offspring of God, we ought not to think that the Godhead is like unto gold, or silver, or stone, graven by art and man's device." (Act 17:24-29)

The Third Commandment

"Thou shalt not take the name of the LORD thy God in vain; for the LORD will not hold him guiltless that taketh his name in vain." (Exodus 20:7)

This means that we are not to use the name of God lightly or irreverently. Neither are we to swear by his name as in an oath or witness to the truth. Neither should we use the name of God as a joke or as a curse word. We are commanded not to bear his name in vain, that is, we should not claim to worship and glorify God and yet live a life that is shameful. This is a breaking of that commandment.

Another way in which this commandment is broken is when false preachers rise up to seek to represent the word of God to the people. When they preach and proclaim false doctrine they are certainly taking God's name in vain and bringing a great reproach upon the name and person of God.

This commandment emphasizes the importance of how we speak and the words we use to communicate. Using the terms "I swear to God" when seeking to tell the truth are a great misuse of his name and a reproach. The Scriptures tell us that our yes should be yes and our no be no, anything more is from the evil one. God will hold you accountable before him and he will judge you for your words. Be careful what you say and how you speak for you will not be guiltless when you use God's name in vain.

Fourth Commandment

"8 Remember the sabbath day, to keep it holy. 9 Six days shalt thou labour, and do all thy work: 10 But the seventh day is the sabbath of the LORD thy God: in it thou shalt not do any work, thou, nor thy son, nor thy daughter, thy manservant, nor thy maidservant, nor thy cattle, nor thy stranger that is within thy gates: 11 For in six days the LORD made heaven and earth, the sea, and all that in them is, and rested the seventh day: wherefore the LORD blessed the sabbath day, and hallowed it." (Exodus 20:8-11)

The word sabbath means "rest from labor." God commands us to keep it holy. That is keep it set apart from the rest of the days. It makes you take a break and stop working. This is what God did on the seventh day of creation.

"1 Thus the heavens and the earth were finished, and all the host of them. 2 And on the seventh day God ended his work which he had made; and he rested on the seventh day from all his work which he had made. 3 And God blessed the seventh day, and sanctified it: because that in it he had rested from all his work which God created and made." (Genesis 2:1-3)

We can gather two things from this. One, that God instituted a day of rest for mankind. As Jesus said, *"The sabbath was made for man, and not man for the sabbath."* The sabbath was instituted as a day for man to have bodily rest and to focus his attention and efforts on spiritual matters. God designed a day of rest for our blessing and our mental and spiritual health. This principle applies regardless of the day that it should be recognized on. For the Jews the seventh day was instituted from what we consider Friday evening through the end of the daylight hours on Saturday.

"So then, there remains a Sabbath rest for the people of God," (Hebrews 4:9)

The Sabbath day is a type of the rest for the people of God in heaven. It is not to be literally fulfilled on Friday night to Saturday afternoon. It is a spiritual rest from works of the Law, Christ, having fulfilled the Law and bring forgiveness and rest from our labors. In Galatians 4:9-11 Paul mourns for the Galatians because they were seduced by followers of the Jewish Law and he rebukes them saying, *"Ye observe days, and months, and times, and years!"* He goes on to say he was afraid that he worked so hard to lead them to Christ in vain.

Christians were accustomed to gather together on Sunday, the first day of the week, and worship together because that is the day that the Lord Jesus Christ was raised from the dead. In order to honor the resurrection, believers in Christ gather together around the world on that day. We are not required to follow specific laws as the Jews did regarding these days. If your nation forces you to be unable to follow this then you have to prayerfully consider it, but it is encouraged to make Sunday your day of rest from your labors so that you can rest your body and focus on spiritual things. If your country does not allow you to do this then you have to prayerfully consider all things. Take a day for resting your body and mind. In countries that people do not take this day for resting all manners of disease, poverty, and moral depravity prevail.

Fifth Commandment

"Honour thy father and thy mother: that thy days may be long upon the land which the LORD thy God giveth thee." (Exodus 20:12)

As the apostle Paul says in Ephesians 6:2 this is the first commandment with a promise of blessing attached to it. This command prohibits us from speaking roughly to our parents, acting rudely or dishonestly with them and acting with contempt towards them. It commands us to treat them with kindness, respect and obedience. If your parents become weak, sick or a bad situation befalls them it is your responsibility to do all within your power to care for them. If you need to go on the street to beg for them than that is what you must do.

When you are young your parents are standing in the place of God to train, teach and guide you in life. Rebellion of children against parents is a rebellion against God. The reason for that is that God through providence has given you the parents that you have. A respect, kindness and obedience is to be given to them. Much can be said for how the parents are to handle this responsibility as they stand in the place of God, or rather, are the tool that God uses to train, teach and correct children. A parents job should be taken with great reverence for the position God places us in. The child should be taught the commandments so that

18

they know the truth and are able to live a life after the word of God.

This is not a commandment that has an ending place. While the scripture also states, *"Therefore shall a man leave his father and his mother, and shall cleave unto his wife: and they shall be one flesh."* (Genesis 2:24). Even though we are to leave our parents and make our spouse our closest relationship we are not free from this command. As long as we are living we are to honor our father and mother, that means we have a responsibility to care for them in old age and weakness.

Sixth Commandment

"Thou shalt not kill." (Exodus 20:13)

This commandment prohibits the deliberate killing of another human being. Jesus tells that even hating a person is considered murder. (Matthew 5:21) This commandment forbids anger, malice or any emotion that leads to murder. The word kill in Hebrew means "to put to death, to dash in pieces, to slay" a human being. It also forbids suicide since that is also the taking of the life of a human being, your own life.

This command also prohibits the killing of infants in the womb. In the Old Testament killing an unborn baby was a crime that was connected to the death penalty. While in some cultures killing an unborn baby is women's rights, according to God's eternal truth, abortion is murder and it is commanded against. Those who commit abortion are murders and will be held guilty before God, except they repent and seek forgiveness.

This command also reveals that not only are we guilty if we kill others, but if it is our power to do good to our neighbor and we do not do it we are guilty. We are called upon to protect, feed and defend our neighbor so that no bodily harm comes to him. If a person doesn't have adequate clothing and you do not clothe him you have caused him to freeze to death. If a person does not have any food and you can feed him then you have caused him to starve to death. If a person is wrongfully accused or convicted and you have means to help him and you do not you are guilty.

"Jesus said, "42 For I was an hungred, and ye gave me no meat: I was thirsty, and ye gave me no drink: 43 I was a stranger, and ye took me not in: naked, and ye clothed me not: sick, and in prison, and ye visited me not... 46 And these shall go away into everlasting punishment: but the righteous into life eternal."" (Matthew 25:42-43, 46)

Those who do not care for others will be sent to everlasting punishment. It's God's ultimate purpose with this commandment that we do not allow harm to fall upon our fellow man and that we should protect, feed, clothe and care for him by any and all means possible.

Seventh Commandment

"Thou shalt not commit adultery." (Exodus 20:14)

This commandment forbids sex outside of marriage. The commandment specifically deals with adultery which is when a man sleeps with a married woman, but it also implies that the only place that sex belong is inside of marriage. Outside of marriage sex is a sin and a violation of the seventh commandment. Sex belongs only to a husband and wife who have stood before God and taken vows to be faithful and to honor God together.

"But I [Jesus] say unto you, That whosoever looketh on a woman to lust after her hath committed adultery with her already in his heart." (Matthew 5:28)

Even a lustful look towards a woman you are not married to is considered adultery. And of course a woman that present herself with sensual, immodest dress with her breasts sticking out, tight jeans or dress is guilty with the man of enticing him to lust. Women, do not be guilty of bringing a candle into a room filled with gunpowder. You live among sinners and the husbands and sons of your friends. So order your dress so that you are not enticing them to lust and sin against God. You will not be guiltless.

Let me say it again, all sex outside of marriage between a man and a woman is a violation of the seventh commandment. It wise not only to avoid sex outside of marriage, but to avoid the temptation as well. Do not go into the room or home of a man or woman alone. Do not kiss or touch the body of someone who is not your spouse. Avoid sin, but also the temptations that lead to sin.

This command also calls us to honor marriage and in so doing to honor the spouse that God has given to us. We are to be faithful to our spouse and to love, honor and cherish them. Treat them with kindness, care and do all within our power to do good to them.

The Eighth Commandment

"Thou shalt not steal." (Exodus 20:15)

This commandment forbids the taking of someone's else's property. It also condemns slavery, kidnapping, private and government stealing. Withholding the rights of individuals and groups is forbidden by the command. It also forbids taking someone else's property or money with fraud. If one makes false promises and does not fulfill the promises he is stealing and violating the eighth commandment.

This command shows that we have the right to own property and that neither individuals or the government have the divine right to take away what belongs to us. While it does belong to us it does not mean that we should cling to it and not use it to do good unto others. However, the government nor other individuals have the right to steal it away and give it to others or keep it for themselves. Seizure of our rightful property is forbidden and is a sin.

Through the sixth commandment God protects our person by commanding that we should not kill. Through the seventh commandment God protects our relationship with our spouse by commanding that we should not commit adultery. Through the eighth commandment he protects our property by commanding that we should not steal. God's commands are not merely to tell us what not to do, but to protect us and keep us from harm.

The practice of laziness at a job or wasting of your business time is forbidden because through your laziness you have stolen money from your employer. Taking items that belong to your employer without their consent is stealing as well; bringing paper clips, pens, paper and other supplies home without the consent of your employer is stealing from them.

Ninth Commandment

"Thou shalt not bear false witness against thy neighbour." (Exodus 20:16)

This commandment deals directly with telling lies in an official inquiry or in a court hearing. God commands us to speak the truth in matters of official business, but also in day to day life. This also forbids us to gossip, tell stories about, slander, talk behind people's back, spread rumors, give little secret hints and in general speak against your neighbor.

This commandment is given to protect our character and the character of others by condemning the rampant practice of gossip and lying. God demands that we tell the truth and he will hold us accountable at the day of judgement if we are found to be liars. Though lying is acceptable in certain circumstances in some cultures, the God of the universe tells us lying is a sin and will be judged. As the Bible says, *"...all liars, shall have their part in the lake which burneth with fire and brimstone: which is the second death."* (Revelation 21:8)

Judges, government officials, managers, CEO's, pastors and all people of authority have to take earnest heed to this. Your word and your witness against or for others carries great weight. You must be careful to always be a true witness. If you bear false witness you can destroy someone's life. They can lose their job, ruin their character, cause them to feel injured or abused, etc. Indeed, each one of us has the potential to ruin someone's character and fortune in life by our words. Every word we speak is heard by God and recorded in a book. We will be judged by them.

"36 But I say unto you, That every idle word that men shall speak, they shall give account thereof in the day of judgment. 37 For by thy words thou shalt be justified, and by thy words thou shalt be condemned." (Matthew 12:36-37)

Tenth Commandment

"Thou shalt not covet thy neighbour's house, thou shalt not covet thy neighbour's wife, nor his manservant, nor his maidservant, nor his ox, nor his ass, nor any thing that is thy neighbour's." (Exodus 20:17)

The word covet means to desire or to long after. The commandments not only condemn outward sins, but inward sins, sins of the thought life. The word covet is closely linked with the word lust and speaks of a delight and earnest desire to possess something that does not belong to you. We are not to earnestly desire anything that does not belong to us. The commandments not only forbid adultery, killing and stealing, but also the desire that leads to these acts.

We learn from this command that we are to be content with what we have now. This does not mean that we cannot work hard and earn the right to purchase something. Rather, it tells us that we should live our lives in a way that we are content with whatever we have. If we are able to purchase a new car or to find a wife to marry or find a new home that is not a sin. The sin is when we see our neighbor have good things and we begin to become jealous and we desire to have what he has. We desire to acquire for ourselves what belongs to another.

This also forbids those who would using a crafty plan would legally acquire that which belongs to another man. This happens when there is a lawsuit over an inheritance or real estate. As Paul wrote, *"Now therefore there is utterly a fault among you, because ye go to law one with another. Why do ye not rather take wrong? why do ye not rather suffer yourselves to be defrauded?"* (1 Corinthians 6:7) The wealthy and government officials find themselves in this position. Using their position and wealth they can acquire property using legal means. Yet when this is done because of coveting your neighbor's possessions it is forbidden.

Conclusions on the Ten Commandments

These are commands of God not suggestions or good ideas. We are not "under the law" and yet these laws are applicable to all of mankind because God will hold them accountable for them. These are laws that we will be judged by and therefore being "under grace" we are given the power through the Holy Spirit to overcome and so avoid violating the 10 commandments and sin. We have the strength through the grace of the Spirit of God to overcome sin. We cannot use grace as an excuse to sin.

UNDERSTANDING GOD

Who is GOD?

Another important aspect of following God and is knowing who is and knowing who he is not. In order to understand who God is we must refer to the authority of the Bible. The Bible is the place that God has chosen to reveal himself to mankind through. We cannot take only the parts of the Bible that we like, but we have to look at the whole of Scripture. Let's examine this closely. We start with John 4:24 where Jesus tells us that *"God is a Spirit."* That means that he is not made up of flesh and blood. The word Spirit in both Hebrew and Greek means wind. God is a person so he is not merely energy or wind. Yet, he is described like wind because he is invisible and he is a person that is all powerful, all knowing and present everywhere.

God is One

The greatest command of the Bible according to the Lord Jesus Christ is that the Lord God is one. As we read through chapters like Isaiah 44 and Ephesians 1 we discover that God is constantly spoke of with a singular personal pronoun. The starting point for all our endeavors is that

God is one. God is not two or three. There is only one God and as the first commandment tells us we are to have no other gods before him. He alone is God and there is none besides him or before him.

"That they may know from the rising of the sun, and from the west, That there is none beside me. I am the LORD, and there is none else." (Isaiah 45:6)

God Revealed In Three Aspects

"The grace of the Lord Jesus Christ, and the love of God, and the communion of the Holy Ghost, be with you all. Amen." (2 Corinthians 13:14)

In this verse we see the New Testament revelation; the Lord Jesus Christ, God and the Holy Spirit. Matthew 28:19 speaks of Father, Son and the Holy Spirit. There are three that are spoken of here, but we must find out what kind of threeness that is referenced. Let's find another reference to the three.

"But he, being full of the Holy Ghost, looked up stedfastly into heaven, and saw the glory of God, and Jesus standing on the right hand of God." (Acts 7:55)

First we have Stephen full of the Holy Spirit, next we have the glory of God and thirdly we have Jesus standing on the right hand of God. God is a Spirit as we started with and he is one. The glory of God is a reference to the supernatural light that was often seen by prophets and priests in the Old Testament. When Solomon's temple of God was built and dedicated the glory of God came down and entered into the holiest of holies. The glory of God is an expression of the personal presence of the one true and living God. The Holy Spirit is referred to as the power of the Highest (Luke 1:35) and proceeds from the Father (John 15:26). The Spirit that comes forth from the Father to dwell in and live in men and women. Jesus, of course, is the Son of God (Luke 1:35) who is the *"image of the invisible God"* (Colossians 1:15) and when you have seen Jesus you have *"seen the Father"* (John 14:9).

Father, Son and Spirit are three different aspects of God's being. Humans are made in the image and likeness of God. (Genesis 1:26-27) We are also made up of body, soul and spirit. (Hebrews 4:12) Just as these are three aspects of our being so is Father, Son and Spirit three aspects of God's one being.

The Father is God

"Jesus answered, If I honour myself, my honour is nothing: it is my Father that honoureth me; of whom ye say, that he is your God:" (John 8:54)

"And this is life eternal, that they might know thee the only true God, and Jesus Christ, whom thou hast sent." (John 17:3)

"But to us there is but one God, the Father, of whom are all things, and we in him; and one Lord Jesus Christ, by whom are all things, and we by him." (1 Corinthians 8:6)

"Grace be to you, and peace, from God our Father, and from the Lord Jesus Christ." (Ephesians 1:2)

"Blessed be the God and Father of our Lord Jesus Christ, who hath blessed us with all spiritual blessings in heavenly places in Christ:" (Ephesians 1:3)

"That the God of our Lord Jesus Christ, the Father of glory, may give unto you the spirit of wisdom and revelation in the knowledge of him:" (Ephesians 1:17)

"Jesus saith unto her, Touch me not; for I am not yet ascended to my Father: but go to my brethren, and say unto them, I ascend unto my Father, and your Father; and to my God, and your God." (John 20:17)

All these verses first identify that the Father is God and Jesus identifies him as his God and the only true God. This is important to understand that the Father is the Godhead, he is the source and the fountain of Deity. Jesus as the human Son of God tells us that his Father is his God and our God.

Jesus is God Manifested

"And without controversy great is the mystery of godliness: God was manifest in the flesh, justified in the Spirit, seen of angels, preached unto the Gentiles, believed on in the world, received up into glory." (1 Timothy 3:16)

Jesus is God manifest in the flesh, he is the visible appearance of God and the glory of God made flesh. We discussed the Father, Son and Spirit in a previous section. Let's look more closely at this. I want to see exactly who was dwelling in Jesus and how was he God.

"How God anointed Jesus of Nazareth with the Holy Ghost and with power: who went about doing good, and healing all that were oppressed of the devil; for God was with him." (Acts 10:38)

So according to the will and act of God Jesus was anointed with the Holy Ghost and this was proven by the good works he did to raise the dead, cast out devils, heal the sick and tell people who they were. So the Holy Ghost was in Jesus. Next, let's look at John 14.

"7 If ye had known me, ye should have known my Father also: and from henceforth ye know him, and have seen him. 8 Philip saith unto him, Lord, shew us the Father, and it sufficeth us. 9 Jesus saith unto him, Have I been so long time with you, and yet hast thou not known me, Philip? he that hath seen me hath seen the Father; and how sayest thou then, Shew us the Father? 10 Believest thou not that I am in the Father, and the Father in me? the words that I speak unto you I speak not of myself: but the Father that dwelleth in me, he doeth the works. 11 Believe me that I am in the Father, and the Father in me: or else believe me for the very works' sake." (John 14:7–11)

Jesus tells his disciples that the works that he did identified that the Father was dwelling in him. But not only that they showed that when you saw Jesus you were seeing the Father. Jesus is the Father made visible in human flesh. So Jesus is the Son of God and dwelling in him was the Father who is a Spirit. So all aspects of God were in Jesus Christ. *"For in him dwelleth all the fulness of the Godhead bodily."* (Colossians 2:9) Father, Son and Spirit are all revealed in the Lord Jesus Christ. *"For it pleased the Father that in him should all fulness dwell."* (Colossians 1:19)

Jesus is the Christ, the Son of God is the revelation

upon which the church is built. (Matthew 16:15-18) To properly understand this revelation we must know there is only one God and he is one person (Galatians 3:20). He is a Spirit and is referred to as the Father because he is the originator and protector and provider for the human race and specifically he directly created Jesus in the womb of Mary. This same Father who is a Spirit lived in and manifested himself through Jesus Christ. So, in Christ dwells all the fulness of the Godhead. Jesus is the body of God and therefore we teach that Jesus Christ is God. He is fully God and fully human.

Father, Son and Holy Spirit are not three gods or three separate individuals like Peter, James and John. This is belief in three gods and is condemned by Scriptures as polytheism. Father, Son and Spirit are three aspects of the same God who is one being. God can be described as the sun, its light and the heat it produces. This is all aspects of the sun itself. The Father is the source, the sun itself, the Son is the light that the sun produces and the Holy Spirit is the heat that is felt upon the earth. Or as man is described as body, soul and spirit so is God Father, Son and Spirit.

THREE ORDINANCES

There are three external ordinances that the Lord Jesus left for us to follow. The first being baptism, then the Lord's Supper and lastly foot washing. Let's look at the purpose of baptism.

Baptism

Baptism is from the term immersing. Baptism was employed by the Jews during temple worship and was used as a form of cleansing prior to engaging in temple work or for worshippers who were coming to offer a sacrifice. This was sometimes the practice for those coming to the synagogues. John the Baptist employed this as a sign of repentance and accepting his message. The term in common usage for baptism was used in regards to immersing a vegetable in vinegar in order to pickle it. It is clear in order to pickle something it must be fully immersed in the vinegar. Otherwise the the vegetable would not be fully pickled. In Romans 6:4 Paul speaks of baptism as a burial. Have you ever heard of a person that was buried who was only sprinkled with a little dirt on their head? This is the tradition of Orthodox, Lutheran and other Reformed churches. They sprinkle infants or adult believers with water. This is contrary to both the normal usage of the term baptism and to the picture that the apostle Paul offers of baptism.

"¹⁵ And he said unto them, Go ye into all the world, and preach the gospel to every creature. ¹⁶ He that believeth and is baptized shall be saved; but he that believeth not shall be damned." (Mark 16:15-16)

This is Jesus' instructions to his disciples before he was caught up to heaven. They were to go into all the world and proclaim the gospel and for those who believe they were to be immersed in water in the singular name of the Father, Son and Spirit.

"Then Peter said unto them, Repent, and be baptized every one of you in the name of Jesus Christ for the remission of sins, and ye shall receive the gift of the Holy Ghost." (Acts 2:38)

While in Matthew 28:19 Jesus commanded his disciples to baptize new converts in the NAME of the Father and of the Son and of the Holy Spirit Peter commands converts to be baptized in the name of Jesus Christ. Peter is following closely the words of Jesus Christ and baptizing them in the NAME, which is Jesus Christ.

"And whatsoever ye do in word or deed, do all in the name of the Lord Jesus, giving thanks to God and the Father by him." (Colossians 3:17)

"Neither is there salvation in any other: for there is none other name under heaven given among men, whereby we must be saved." (Acts 4:12)

We are called upon to do everything that we do in the name of the Lord Jesus and that his name is the only name given among men whereby we must be saved. So when Jesus says baptize in the NAME he is showing that he NAME of the Father, Son and Spirit is the Lord Jesus Christ. As both history and the book of Acts bear record, new converts, after repentance and confession of faith you are to be baptized in the name of the Lord Jesus Christ. Jesus did not say baptize in the NAMES, plural, Father, Son and Spirit, but the one NAME that belongs to the Father, the Son and the Spirit which is Jesus Christ. This should be done by total immersion by a clean and godly minister of the gospel.

The Lord's Supper

The same night that Jesus was betrayed he gathered together his disciples and they ate a meal together. They ate bread and drank wine. During this time Jesus instituted what we call the Lord's Supper.

"23 For I have received of the Lord that which also I delivered unto you, That the Lord Jesus the same night in which he was betrayed took bread: 24 And when he had given thanks, he brake it, and said, Take, eat: this is my body, which is broken for you: this do in remembrance of me. 25 After the same manner also he took the cup, when he had supped, saying, This cup is the new testament in my blood: this do ye, as oft as ye drink it, in remembrance of me. 26 For as often as ye eat this bread, and drink this cup, ye do shew the Lord's death till he come. 27 Wherefore whosoever shall eat this bread, and drink this cup of the Lord, unworthily, shall be guilty of the body and blood of the Lord. 28 But let a man examine himself, and so let him eat of that bread, and drink of that cup. 29 For he that eateth and drinketh

unworthily, eateth and drinketh damnation to himself, not discerning the Lord's body. 30 For this cause many are weak and sickly among you, and many sleep. 31 For if we would judge ourselves, we should not be judged." (1 Corinthians 11:23–31)

Jesus took the bread and he broke it. This bread was an unleavened bread, it was without yeast. A flat bread was taken and he broke it and distributed it to his disciples and he told them that the bread was his body that was to be broken for them. He also took the cup and said it was the new testament in his blood. Both times he informed that they were to take it in remembrance of him. Serving and receiving the Lord's supper is a time of great reverence and solemn reflection. We are giving and receiving the Lord's supper to remember his death for our sins. Nowhere does Scripture tells us that the bread and the wine somehow magically turn into the literal body or blood of Jesus. It is literal bread and wine and they are to symbolize that Jesus died for our sins, his flesh was broken and his blood was shed. We eat them to symbolize that we are personal beneficiaries of his death.

The way that the Lord's supper should be taken is in a spirit of judging ourselves, this of course, is a solemn time. It means we are examining our hearts, our attitudes, how we act and feel towards others and to ask God to search our hearts to see if there are any sins we have committed against him or his people. It is not to be taken lightly or with an attitude of not caring. When we take it with a joke and a laugh, doing it lightly we are eating and drinking damnation to ourselves. Prior to drinking of the cup and eating of the bread there should be time for all in the local assembly to prayerfully consider and confess their own sins to God and

34

to examine their own lives and hearts. Treat this time as solemn. The Lord's supper should be served by the local pastors along with deacons or if it is a new church plant with mature believers who the ministry agrees are walking closely in obedience and reverence before God.

The Lord's supper is similar to what in the Old Testament was considered the Passover celebration. This was to be done at night. So, should the Lord's supper be taken together with the church in the evening time. The bread should be unleavened and prayed over by the deacons and pastor. If it all possible it is best that the wine should be made at home by the pastor or one appointed by him. This should also be prayed over.

Foot Washing

"2 And supper being ended, the devil having now put into the heart of Judas Iscariot, Simon's son, to betray him; 3 Jesus knowing that the Father had given all things into his hands, and that he was come from God, and went to God; 4 He riseth from supper, and laid aside his garments; and took a towel, and girded himself. 5 After that he poureth water into a bason, and began to wash the disciples' feet, and to wipe them with the towel wherewith he was girded. 6 Then cometh he to Simon Peter: and Peter saith unto him, Lord, dost thou wash my feet? 7 Jesus answered and said unto him, What I do thou knowest not now; but thou shalt know hereafter." (John 13:2-7)

The key words to understand this is an ordinance of the church is "what I do you know not now, but you shall know after this." Foot washing should be done separately between the sexes, men together and women together in another area. There should be a basin and a towel for foot washing. The feet would be washed and the men would pray for each other. This is a symbol of our service to one another, following the example of the Lord Jesus Christ. It is typically done after the Lord's supper as is shown above in verse 2.

"25 But Jesus called them unto him, and said, Ye know that the princes of the Gentiles exercise dominion over them, and they that are great exercise authority upon them. 26 But it shall not be so among you: but whosoever will be great among you, let him be your minister; 27 And whosoever will be chief among you, let him be your servant: 28 Even as the Son of man came not to be ministered unto, but to minister, and to give his life a ransom for many." (Matthew 20:25-28)

Foot washing is a picture of what the highest virtue is and that is to serve others not to be lord over others and controlling them, but to live in such a way that you are meeting the needs of others. Foot washing cannot be the only outward expression of serving others, but it must be a place we start with in humility being at the feet of our brothers to serve and care for them.

PRAYER

Prayer is not merely one of the outward "forms" that a Christian follows. Prayer is the lifeblood of a believer. Prayer is how we connect directly to God in the worship, relationship and fellowship that he designed and purposed for man. Worship and fellowship is the reason that God created man. Therefore, prayer is our highest purpose in life.

Jesus Christ is not just our example, he is our Lord and Master and yet he is our example for he lived a perfect life. Let's look and find out how and when Jesus prayed.

Jesus Teaches Us How You Pray

"And when he had sent the multitudes away, he went up into a mountain apart to pray: and when the evening was come, he was there alone." (Matthew 14:23)

Jesus went away to a secluded place to pray, he was alone without the company of others and he spent a long time in prayer through the evening. He did not merely spend a short time, a few minutes, but hours in prayer alone with God. *"And when he had sent them away, he departed into a mountain to pray."* (Mark 6:46)

Here again he went alone into a solitary place in order to pray. The word prayer means to worship, to make requests known and to meditate.

"And it came to pass in those days, that he went out into a mountain to pray, and continued all night in prayer to God. And when it was day, he called unto him his disciples: and of them he chose twelve, whom also he named apostles." (Luke 6:12-13)

Here Jesus had a big decision to make in his life and he needed to be sure of what he should do. So, in order to do that he went away, by himself, into a secluded place and he prayed all night long. You say it's impossible to do such a thing, but if you are desperate for God it certainly is not.

"28 And it came to pass about an eight days after these sayings, he took Peter and John and James, and went up into a mountain to pray. 29 And as he prayed, the fashion of his countenance was altered, and his raiment was white and glistering." (Luke 9:28-29)

Jesus took with him three of his apostles and they went together up into a mountain to pray. As he was praying he had a great experience with God; the presence of God came and his face and garments began to radiate with the glory of God. For us, we may not have experiences like this when we pray, but when we do, very often the presence of God comes to us in such a way that it changes our hearts and strengthens us for the day and trials ahead. We meet God when we pray.

Paul's Commands

"I will therefore that men pray every where, lifting up holy hands, without wrath and doubting." (1 Timothy 2:8)

Paul desired that we pray everywhere, not merely at church services, but at all times and in every place. He said to do it lifting up holy hands, that is, raising your hands in request to God. And we are called to pray without anger, that is to pray with a good attitude towards our fellow man and as you pray to not have a spirit of anger or bad feelings towards fellow man. He also tells them to pray without doubting. This means to pray with reliance and faith in the promises of God, not to pray with timidity and full of reasonings against God and his Word.

"¹ I exhort therefore, that, first of all, supplications, prayers, intercessions, and giving of thanks, be made for all men; ² For kings, and for all that are in authority; that we may lead a quiet and peaceable life in all godliness and honesty." (1 Timothy 2:1-2)

Paul says we should pray for all men and he mentions several specific kinds of prayer; supplicants which is prayer for averting evils, prayers which means prayers for spiritual and natural blessings, and intercessions which are prayers on behalf of others and giving of thanks which is praising God for all his goodness, blessings and glory. And he says to pray not only for all men, but also for your government leaders and officials so that we can lead a quiet and peaceable life. There was a persecution arising at the time in the Roman Empire against Christians and instead of Paul saying the government is from the devil and don't pray for them he says instead that we should pray for them.

39

"13 And whatsoever ye shall ask in my name, that will I do, that the Father may be glorified in the Son. 14 If ye shall ask any thing in my name, I will do it." (John 14:13-14)

Here we find that Jesus tells us to ask in prayer in his name. So we are to approach God in the name of Jesus Christ. Next let's look at the prayer that Jesus used as an example, what we call the Lord's Prayer.

The Lord's Prayer

"9 After this manner therefore pray ye: Our Father which art in heaven, Hallowed be thy name. 10 Thy kingdom come. Thy will be done in earth, as it is in heaven. 11 Give us this day our daily bread. 12 And forgive us our debts, as we forgive our debtors. 13 And lead us not into temptation, but deliver us from evil: For thine is the kingdom, and the power, and the glory, for ever. Amen." (Mat 6:9-13)

This is not to be a prayer we simply memorize and repeat, though that practice is fine, instead it is a prayer that is an example of how we should approach God.

First, we approach God as "our Father" that is he is in relationship with us as a Father and as such he seeks our fellowship and our good. To be a Father means that he is our source of life, he is our provider and our teacher. He is our Father who is in heaven, he is above us, the God that created all things, that controls and directs all things.

The first petition is asking that God's name be holy or set apart from all others. The next petition is that his kingdom would come to earth, his rule, his authority would come. The third petition is that his will, his purpose, would be fulfilled on earth as it is in heaven. He is the sovereign ruler of heaven and earth and yet our desire should be for his plan to be fulfilled on earth.

The first approach we make to God in prayer is regarding him and his purposes. We worship him, honor him and give him praise as we begin to approach him in prayer. Then after we praise him and confess his glory and greatness and pray for his purposes to be fulfilled, for people to be saved, lives to be changed, the gospel to go to the nations, etc. we make our personal requests known such as "our daily bread" and the financial needs we have, the needs for family members, needs for strength and to make our heart known to God.

After this he tells us to ask for forgiveness for our sins. In prayer we should allow God to search our hearts and to ourselves search our hearts to see if there be any sin and confess this sin to God and in turn forgive the sins of others against us. If we do not forgive those who sin against us our Father in heaven will not forgive our sins. The disposition of our heart should be humility, recognizing we need forgiveness and because of that granting forgiveness to those that have wronged us in word or in deed.

Then he says, "lead us not into temptation, but deliver us from evil." Temptation here means a trial. It means that we are praying that God keeps us from trials that we cannot bear and from people that cause us to sin. This is a prayer for protection from this trials that so easily lead us astray. It's both protection from and deliverance through, that is strength to bear the trial without falling away from faith.

41

"For thine is the kingdom, and the power, and the glory, for ever. Amen." This is the ending of prayer and it shows we should again give worship to God, begin the prayer with worship and praise and end your prayer with worship and praise. It signifies, all things belong to you, O God, and you have the power to answer my prayers, deliver me, provide food and raiment, money to pay our debts, power to forgive our sins and grant us peace.

In summary prayer is a fellowship and worship to God; it is our lifeblood as Christians. It is not a side note or a nice thing to do sometimes, but the disposition of our hearts should be to pray at all times and in all places *"lifting up holy hands without wrath or doubting."* (1 Timothy 2:8) Jesus spent hours and full nights in prayer in solitude and with others.

CONCLUSION

It is the will of God for us to grow in faith. This is a good start for the basics of the Christian faith, but in order to continue to grow you need to continue in prayer and the study of the word of God.

"2 Grace and peace be multiplied unto you through the knowledge of God, and of Jesus our Lord, 3 According as his divine power hath given unto us all things that pertain unto life and godliness, through the knowledge of him that hath called us to glory and virtue:" (2 Peter 1:2–3)

Grace and peace can be multiplied, that is, we can grow in grace and peace. We are to increase in grace and peace through the knowledge of him that called us. The sure sign of spiritual death is to stop increasing in this work of grace. Or perhaps it is that you have not yet been born again. In that case you must get on your knees and in desperation ask God to give you the Holy Spirit.

"If ye then, being evil, know how to give good gifts unto your children: how much more shall your heavenly Father give the Holy Spirit to them that ask him?" (Luke 11:13)

Made in the USA
Columbia, SC
13 April 2024

34329656R00024